A GENTLE GUIDE

TO BECOMING

THE BEST FRIEND

YOU CAN BE

Are You My
FRIEND?

MARY DOUGLAS-WITHERSPOON

ARE YOU MY FRIEND?

PROMINENT
BOOKS
EDGE

5830 E 2nd St, Ste 7000 #9983
Casper, WY 82609
USA

DEDICATION

This book is dedicated to my two dearest friends, Joan Werner and Ramona Davis. Thank you for always being there for me. You are my earthly angels.

To my sisters, Sonia, Elizabeth, Naomi and Regina, and my brothers Norton and Paul, who have always been my friends. You have always lifted me up and encouraged me to be who God called me to be. I am grateful to God that we share the same DNA. Love you so much.

To all of those who have loved me and have shown me some level of friendship in my life, I thank you. You have given me the experiences necessary to write this book and understand more about this relationship called "friendship."

CONTENTS

CONTENTS

FOREWORD

I first met my best friend Mary when we were both working and living in New York City. She would buzz around the office singing and smiling and bringing joy to all those around her. She was truly a bright light and loved by all, and she STILL IS!

> *"Here together, friends forever. Some things were just meant to be, and that's you and me."*
>
> —*Winnie the Pooh*

We were both in our twenties at the time. So young, fresh, and ready for the adventures that awaited us and then life happened. And there she was, never giving up on me even when I was giving up on myself. She taught me how to be a true friend without me even knowing. Thank God for my precious friendship with Mary.

"A day without a friend is like a pot without a single drop of honey left inside."

—*Winnie the Pooh*

I cannot imagine going through life without my dear Mary. She is my person—the one who shares my ups and downs. No judgment. No lies. Safe. Loving. The one who lifts me up. The one who tells me the truth. The truth but, always with grace. A blessing. My friend.

"If you live to be 100, I hope I live to be 100 minus one day, so I never have to live without you."

—*Winnie the Pooh*

Friendship is a gift from God. I am so excited you have the opportunity to read this guide and begin to truly understand what this gift really means. Better yet, read this guide with a friend. It will take your relationship to another level. You will truly be blessed.

"A wise bear indeed!"

—*Joan Kitson Werner*

Note from the Author

I've worked in corporate America as an administrative assistant at Chase Bank in New York City and as a police dispatcher for thirty years in Niagara Falls, New York. So, I've lived in the "big city" and what would be seen as a "small city." I've worked with and for a diverse population—rich people, poor people, black people, white people, nice people, not-so-nice people old and young people. What I have come to know is that we all want the same things. We love and want to be loved. Whether it is in a relationship of marriage, family or friends, we want to be loved. And as hard as it is for some people to admit, we want to be liked.

People get married for many different reasons, and family is DNA, but *friends are the ones we choose.* I consider myself a people-watcher, and I have watched the actions of some and wondered why they chose a particular person to be their friend. I have also watched the actions of friends and can point out why their friendship must be working.

I don't consider myself to be an expert on friendship matters, but I do believe I have insight that I have gained in my over sixty-plus years of living that might be interesting and helpful to some. Though this is an easy read and could be read in one sitting, my suggestion is that you read a chapter at a time. Read it, meditate on it, and take in the affirmations in each chapter. Look at your most precious friendships and see how that particular point is working in your life.

Maybe even read it with your friend or friends and see how they feel you all are doing. Open a dialogue that opens your heart even more.

I hope that you receive something from this guide and hopefully it will help you to grow in your friendship.

—Mary

INTRODUCTION

I 've listened to people speak about their friends; what they do and don't do, how they were hurt or blessed by them, and I've heard them excuse bad behavior by saying, "That's just the way they are." as if it was ok. Sometimes they would ask, "Do you think I should say something?", or "What should I do?" People have many questions and want answers. I thought I just might have a few of those answers.

I have two friends I am very close to, Joan and Ramona. We have been through some great times and some tough times together. I have made some mistakes along the way but my hope is that I have learned from them and won't repeat them. Mistakes like being selfish or jealous or being unintentional. Being selfish, as in making something more about me when it should be about them. Being jealous, as in when they spent time with someone else and had a great time without me. Being unintentional, as in not letting them know how much they mean to me. These were hard lessons learned but they were learned.

I had a person read the first draft of this book, and she said there were some things with which she did not agree. I asked her, "Why not?" She said, "I don't think a friend would do some of those things." I immediately defended myself because, after all, this is my *baby*. How could you not like my baby? How could you say my baby wasn't beautiful? But, then, it caused me to pause, and I had to begin to think about it sincerely. So, I began to ponder what I had written. Am I looking for more out of a friend than I should? Was I wrong? Will people think it's too much? I considered changing what I wholeheartedly believed to be, the truth. But I could not. **THIS IS A FRIEND**.

I began to wonder why she would think a friend would not follow this path. It then became more apparent. Not everyone knows what a true friend is. After all, this person was just in her early twenties. True friendship is like the finest wine. It takes time to develop fully. It must be nurtured, cared for, protected, watched over, and shown love. You must be willing to do the work to get it there. But once it's done, it is oh so satisfying. Let's face it, some relationships are not worth the work, but those that are, will become one of life's greatest blessings. People do have true friends in their teens and twenties but they may not know it yet because the relationship hasn't been tested. Isn't it great when we pass a test?

In our lives, we deal with three kinds of relationships outside of our family. They are acquaintances, people we are friendly with and friends. If we get these relationships mixed up or place people in the wrong category, there is potential for hurt, anger, disappointment, and misunderstanding. Often, we have put people in the wrong category.

When we understand what we are dealing with, we know what NOT to expect. We don't go to a chef to talk about foot pain, and we don't go to a mechanic to get our hair done. You'll be soaking your feet in marinara sauce and conditioning your hair with motor oil. The co-worker we are friendly with will probably not end up holding our hair back while we throw up in the toilet, and it probably isn't something we should expect. Otherwise, we will be sorely disappointed. But our *friend* will not only hold our hair back, but they'll also clean us up and put us to bed, then come back in the morning to check on us and keep coming back until they know we are fine. Everyone needs a hair-holding friend!

My best friend lives over 600 miles away from me. When I had become very, very ill and could not get out of my bed she called me three or four times a day. When I had recovered I thanked her for just talking to me while I was sick.

I said "You took time every day to call me. You called so many times a day."

She said "I never wanted you to feel like you were alone." That thought still brings a "love tear" to my eye. This is a friend.

Let's get a better understanding of the three kinds of relationships.

Acquaintances: These are people you see here and there, and have a conversation with, but you know little more than their names and maybe where they work. Perhaps they are even a co-worker. You have no further relationship with them and don't expect any more out of them than a friendly "Hello," and "How's the weather?"

conversation. These are the people you might say, "I know OF them." Sometimes, they've already shown you somehow with their words or actions a glimpse of who they really are, and it makes you say, "I don't want to know any more of them," or "Nope, not going there." Maya Angelou said, "When people show you who they are, believe them."

People you are friendly with: You hear people say, "I've got lots of friends." Most people only have a few "friends" and usually only one or two. Truth is what you *likely* have are a lot of people you are friendly with. These are people you show interest in, some good will towards, and those with whom you may spend a small amount of time. You might sit with them during your kids' games. Maybe you grab a bite to eat together now and then. You might share minor information about each other's lives, about marriage status, kids' information, and your interests, but nothing intimate. These people may or may not have the potential to be friends, but only time will tell. There are times when you realize that being friendly is all you want, and you keep them at arm's length, (but with your nicer arm, of course.) You may call them a friend, but you know the relationship is only on a surface level. You don't expect anything more from them than what you see on the surface, and you're not planning to give more.

Friends: These are the people who know you well. You know the intimate details of each other's lives. They are a part of your life. You know that your innermost thoughts are safe with them. You can be at your best and your worst with them, and they love you the same. They love you, and they LIKE you. They understand you. They know your whys and why nots. They are the people you want to spend time with. They are the ones you want to talk to and be around. You want to laugh with them, cry with them, to discuss the serious and the silly, the real and the ridiculous. You are happy to see them. You are delighted to be with them. This is your friend. This is your gift. This relationship is God-given. This relationship will bless your life. This is who I am writing about. *This is a friend.* What I want you to understand when reading this book is that friendships are ever-evolving. As we grow and change, some of our friendships grow and change with us. Some of them do not. Sometimes, we lose them along the way. But, the friendships that grow and evolve with you fill you with a joy that cannot be measured.

So if you read this and say "I don't do that", look at your relationships and see if you have evolved to that point yet, or strive to be better at one of these points. Friendship is different for everyone because we are at different ages, have different life experiences, and are in different seasons of our lives. But there are some core values for friendship that no matter where you are in this process you should have. I believe three of these values are trust, truth and love. As you read this guide, look at your relationships. Determine who is authentically your friend. Do you need to place people in a different and more suitable category? Are you as good a friend as you thought you were? After every chapter, take a moment, as my brother Norton would say, and "assess your situation."

FRIEND

" Friend" is defined as a person attached to another by feelings or personal regard. It is a mutual regard cherished by kindred minds; a person you know well and regard with affection and trust.[1] I agree with all of that but I would add that I feel a friend is the hand of God reaching down to touch your life.

I read a quote that said, "There are friends in life, and there are friends for life."[2] How true this is! There are people who I believe God put in our lives for just a season because He wants to teach us something or get us through something. They were never meant to stay. They were only there to help us during a specific period in our life and then send us on our way. **Recognize this**. It will help you understand when someone you genuinely cared about is no longer in your life full-time, especially when there was nothing that ended the friendship. It just ended. It ended because the season was

---

[1]   Dictionary.com

[2]   Quotespedia.org (author unknown)

over. Look back and see what you got out of it and what you gave to it. *Side note, there are also people you wish would get out of your life because they have made your season seem waaaayyy too long!* I'm just sayin'…

But there are *friends we have for life.* You are God's gift to one another. A friend's worth cannot be calculated, weighed, or measured. If we are blessed to have a true friend, we have a priceless treasure in our possession, and should be treated as something precious.

When we are young, the premise of friendship may not be completely defined. We are more concerned about peers, peer pressure, and fitting in than who might really be a friend. But, as we grow older and life happens to us, we not only understand the value of friendship, but we see better what the characteristics of a true friend are.

In fact, God calls us friend. (John 15:15) That alone tells me how important friendship is. There is no monetary amount or materialistic gift that can be traded for the value of a friend. A true friend, I believe, is given to you by God. Never take it for granted, and never take it as a coincidence that you are connected to the heart of another. God, Who is omniscient, knows what we need before we need it. Therefore, He has molded and crafted someone to fit a purpose designed just for you.

Friends share a love that is pure, honest, and blessed. I am so grateful to God that He has given me a little understanding of this relationship called friendship. As much as I believe I know, I find I am still learning the wonder of it all and the work in it all. I am even more grateful that God has given me a couple friends that live up to this wonder.

We were never meant to travel our life's journey alone. God gives us people who hear our heart, understand our journey, and walk along with us. So, hold hands with someone. This is the will of God. Be open to this.

CHAPTER 1

Thou Shall Always Tell The Truth

"Fake friends tell you the pretty lies while, true friends tell you the ugly truth"

—Arpandeep Kaur

Truth is a tie that binds
friendship together.

To tell the truth or not, that is the question. Sometimes, we think we will save our friend's feelings by not being forthcoming. After all, we don't want to hurt the one we love. We don't want to be the one that causes pain. But the reason this is rule number one is because although it may not be easy sometimes, it's imperative to tell the truth to your friend. You should be able to look your friend in the eye and know that whatever you are telling each other is the absolute truth. Respect them enough, to be honest. This is how trust is built. "Faithful are the wounds of a friend, but the kisses of an enemy are deceitful." (Prov. 27:6). These wounds can be trusted because they come from a place of loving and caring, not judging. Someone who always ignores what is awry in your life or where you might be deficient and only giving you compliments and accolades is an enemy to your growth. We want to be the best person we can and having a person always smothering us with kisses does not make way for that to happen. We have to be able to look at our flaws and faults honestly and strive to eliminate them.

A friend wants the same for us. They are willing to cause a wound if it means helping you become the best version of yourself. But a friend is never malicious and takes care in how they present what is necessary to help. I have always said that presentation is *everything*. If we want people to receive what we are saying, we must present it the right way. Giving someone a gourmet meal on a dirty plate will not be well received at all. They might notice the fabulous food, but their attention will be on the dirty dish, and they most likely won't eat it. If they do, I say move this person to the acquaintance category because that is unacceptable behavior!

Sometimes the truth hurts, yet there is no way around it. But the pain of a lie from a friend cannot be measured and can be more harmful than any truth could ever be. No matter what the situation, you should be able to trust the word of your friend. In a world where deception reigns, and where it is much easier to tell a lie than to deal with the trouble of the truth, the honesty of a friend can be life-giving—maybe even lifesaving.

I was talking to my grandchildren about this. At the time, they were ages seven and ten.

I asked them, "If your friend needed to know something about themselves and that information might hurt their feelings, would you tell them the truth?"

While the seven year old pondered it a moment, the ten year old said, "I think you should tell them."

I asked, "Why?"

He said, "Because you should always tell your friend the truth."

The seven year old finally spoke up and said, "No, don't tell them."

I asked, "Why?"

She said, "Because you don't want to hurt their feelings."

Meanwhile, their father chimes in and says "I was thinking you always have to tell your friend the truth, but then you don't want to hurt their feelings."

I had to smile at it all because this is how anyone who genuinely cares about their friend feels. *"What do I do?"* This is the hundred-thousand-dollar question. I have forever said that the truth always rises to the top. It may take a while, but it will rise, and it will eventually be known. So, ask yourself, when that truth rises, where do you want to be found? The thought of being found guilty of not being honest with my friend or having been in some way deceitful makes me physically ill.

So here is an uncomfortable example: You and your friend are going out for the night. She's dressed like a hoochie, or he's dressed like a 1970's pimp, and they ask you, "How do I look?" as they proceed to put their coat on like it's time to go. You must stop and just say, "NO." Be honest. Tell the truth. "You look like a hoochie," or "You look like Rooster from the TV show Baretta." You want to say it before other people do. I can't speak to their reaction. They may not change, they may not care, but as a friend of mine would say, "At least now you know."

If a friend asks you if they are wrong in what they said or did, and they were, tell them the truth. If they ask you if you think the person they are dating is a jerk and they are, tell them the truth. If they ask if they can sing, dance, or play an instrument and they can't, tell them the truth. Just preface every statement with, *"Because I love you, I need to tell you the truth."* Be supportive in any way you can. "No, you can't sing like Kelly Clarkson, and you don't dance like Derrick Huff from *Dancing with the Stars*, but let's do karaoke and go dancing anyway."

Now let's assess your situation. Have you held on to a truth you think your friend should know? Are you wanting to say something but afraid of the hurt it may cause? Weigh it out. Is it something important to the well-being of your friend? Is your friend thinking something is a certain way but it isn't? Will the truth cause a temporary pain but in the end make things better? You have to answer all of these questions. There is no absolute answer that works for everyone. The bottom line is that when you do open your mouth, *let it be the truth.*

CHAPTER 2

Thou Shall Never Tell the Secrets of a Friend

"Confidentiality is the essence of being trusted."

—Billy Graham

Truth and trust are simply a must.

Oh, the secrets of our friends. To have, and to hold them. When a person trusts you enough to give you their secret, they have opened the door to friendship. The walls of privacy have come down and the invitation to come in to their intimate space has been made. To tell their secret to you is to say, "I trust you." Every good relationship is bound together by the strings of trust. Before you walk through that door, take your shoes off, and check to make sure your feet are clean because you are about to walk on holy ground!

Secrets are like precious gems, but the secret itself is not as precious as the holding of the secret. Not everyone gets to hold them. It's said that a secret is something that should be hidden from others, or information known only to a special group. YOU are the special group. You're the inner circle. You're the trusted one. Sometimes a friend just needs someone else to know and you are their safe place. *Let's hope they're not about to tell you they murdered someone.*

I must admit that many years ago, I was asked not to tell a certain secret, and I did. I have never fully recovered from the feeling I got when they realized I had betrayed their trust. When I think of it to this day, I feel a twinge in my stomach. It was nothing life changing or mind blowing or even, in my mind anything that needed to be a secret. But it was a secret for them, and I told it.

Basically, a friend, I will call her Tonya and I were talking about an issue she was having and she told me not to tell a mutual friend, who I will call Lacey. The issue wasn't life changing but it was something Tonya did not want Lacey to know her feelings on.

A few days later I was talking to Lacey and she brought this issue up. Without even thinking, I said, "Well Tonya said this…" As soon as the words came out of my mouth, I thought, *Why did you say that?* and my heart began to beat hard. I really did not mean to tell her secret. Evidently, Lacey went to speak with Tonya about this issue and how she was feeling. The next time Tonya and I were together she said "You told Lacey what I said." She did not say it in anger at all, she said it with disappointment. Oh, that hurt. I might have been able to handle anger better. Of course I apologized with everything in me. But I felt like the damage was done, and asked myself, *"How do I come back from this?"* I wondered for a long time if Tonya would ever trust me again. That is a feeling I never, ever, ever, want to have again. We both came out of that situation feeling hurt. It was a trust betrayed.

Betrayal is hard to recover from. It takes work. But a good friendship is worth the work. Tonya and I have since mended that breach, but it took time and work. Time for her, and work for me. The only exception for breaking trust or telling a secret is when it is connected to preserving someone's health, safety, or sometimes, their life. You can't make the mistake I did. Also, you can't go with "This is not important" or "This other person needs to know". What is important to your friend should hold some weight with you. The trust given to you should hold some weight with you. So, when you find yourself in this situation you have to weigh things out. What will the consequences of telling or not telling be? Weigh very carefully. The "friend secret" is another bond that glues friends together. Well, maybe not every friendship has a deep dark secret but...do you?

Another question we may want to ask is "Why is this a secret?" and do we need to nudge our friend gently into bringing this issue to light? Sometimes when a person is in the middle of something, they can't always clearly see the best way to handle things. Thank God for friends who may be able to see much clearer than you.

The most important thing to remember is it's not the secret, it's the trust. It's not *what you are holding*. It's that *YOU* are holding it. Don't drop it.

Now let's assess your situation: Have you told a secret whether intentionally or accidently? If you have, have you sincerely apologized? Never make an excuse for the wrong you have done while apologizing. Maybe, later you can explain yourself but never give the impression that the reason for them keeping the secret is unnecessary or unimportant. You were trusted, and you broke the trust. Now you must build that trust back, if possible. If you're thinking about telling a secret, be honest about your reason for telling. Will it be a help or will it be a betrayal? I say again, weigh this decision *very carefully*.

CHAPTER 3

Thou Shall Never Disappear on a Friend

"A best friend is one who won't leave you at any point in life, no matter how hard or what it takes to be there"

—Unknown

Truth, trust and staying in touch

Disappearing? "Why would you do that?" Have you ever heard the term "ghosting"? It's when someone cuts off communication without any explanation. They don't answer phone calls, texts, emails, or a knock at the door. I will tell you this if, I knock on my friend's door and she doesn't answer, and I know she is in there, you better believe we have a problem. To just disappear and leave your friend in the dark about where you are, what you are doing, or what you are going through, is unacceptable. It really is. No, seriously, it really is.

In those times of frustration, disappointment, or despair, we may feel the need to get away from everyone and everything. Sometimes we "need a moment." This may or may not be understood by all. But not telling the one you trust, the one who has your back and who probably understands what you are going through better than most that you need that moment, is "cause to pause." I say "pause", because you must think about why you would not tell your friend what is going on. Is it that you don't want a voice of reason? I know there are times we don't. Sometimes we want to be reckless or mysterious, or maybe we are just trying to figure it out ourselves and not bother anyone.

I have a close friend who likes to shut herself away when she is going through a difficult time. In the beginning stages of our friendship, she couldn't be reached. I would call, leave messages, and she wouldn't call back. She would then eventually call and say what had been going on and why it took her a while to get back to me. She has since learned it doesn't work that way. You call back and say, "Things are difficult right now. I need a little time. I don't want to talk about it right now. I need a moment." Granted, you may not want to talk about every little detail of your life. For instance, you may not want to talk about having to go to a Fat Camp because your underwear doesn't fit any more, but at least let your friend know you're going to go away for a week "on a solo vacation."

Whether for a day or a few days, to just disappear without notice is much cause for concern. The care a friend has for you causes them to have your best interest at heart. For your friend to know where you are, and understand what you are doing is important in your relationship and eliminates much stress for them. I'm talking about friends here, not acquaintances. Acquaintances may wonder if you are okay, but friends are going to find out if you are okay. They're going to see about you.

Maybe, before you take your "moment," why not speak with your friend? Often they can see the situation better than you can. Disappearing may be seen as a form of pulling away, but a friend shouldn't pull away in times of distress—they should come closer, and that's on *both sides of the friendship*. Sometimes you just need to hear your friend say, "It's gonna be alright." I have sat many times with my friend and had long conversations about things that were troubling me and how I just wanted to run away. But, after those conversations, things seemed better. She understood where I was because she knew me, and she could see my situation more clearly than I could. And if I needed a moment for real, she was supportive. You should trust your friend enough not to run away from them. I can't emphasize this enough. *Trust is so important.* If you build this, don't break it. When you have worked on creating a strong foundation of trust, don't cause it to fall. It may save your life one day or at least save your sanity. Like I said, disappearing—why would you do that?!

Can I emphasize enough the importance of communication? Talk, talk, talk! It keeps a flow of understanding, and you might find that your friend wants to disappear with you. In that case, it's not disappearing, it's considered time away with friends.

I was watching a series on Netflix called *"Sweet Magnolias"*. It's about three good friends. Every week they get together and they use the term "pour it out." This meant that it was time to talk about whatever was going on with them. I thought to myself if friends would do that more, they would eliminate so much heartache.

Now let's assess your situation: Did you feel better alone in your struggle, or were you still in a state of worry or sadness? What was the reason you didn't pick up the phone? Picking up the phone and making one call could possibly make everything better. Did you not trust your friend to handle your issue? Did you give them a chance? Were you embarrassed by what you were going through? Your friend is the last person for you to be embarrassed in front of.

CHAPTER 4

Thou Shall Never Be Part of a Practical Joke That Will Humiliate

"Your worst humiliation is only someone else's momentary entertainment."

—Uldis Sprogis

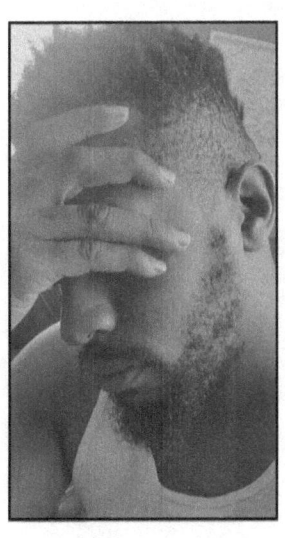

Truth, trust and staying in touch,
with no humiliation to come

Do I need to say a whole lot about this? If you're older than twelve you should understand that practical jokes can sometimes cause humiliation. You can't do that to a friend. It's okay to tease them or play pranks that may cause minor embarrassment, but you must be extremely careful and know where to draw the line. Sometimes it is difficult to come back from a practical joke. What one person thinks is funny may not be funny to another. I have a sister who most times disagrees with what I think is funny. I will tell her things and crack up while I'm telling her, and she is just shaking her head because she doesn't think it's funny at all. I'm thinking *this is hilarious, why aren't you laughing?* At the same time, my youngest sister who is most like me is cracking up. So, you should know your friend. You should know how they will handle a particular joke. If you're not sure, then be sure not to do it.

When people come to you with that "perfect" practical joke to play on your friend, think to yourself, "Perfect for whom?" You might want to pass on it. Others may take something too far, and what was intended as a little folly may turn into something much bigger. You are always to protect your friend from danger AND humiliation. You are your brother's/sister's keeper. In this case, you are the "keeper of the dignity."

Again, depending on what it is, it may not be something easy to come back from. Be very careful of the "perfect practical joke." It just might be filled with flaws. Giving your friend a heads up of what is about to happen may be the best route to take. Some people are quite careless about other people's feelings. Don't let them be that way with the feelings of your friend. Also, consider what the real intentions of others may be? Look, I'm not saying don't have fun with each other. Light-hearted jokes are cool, but when other people come into the scenario, they change the dynamics, and you have to keep a watchful eye to make sure things don't go awry.

I remember a person teasing me about something I did. I laughed along for a while. I could see it as being funny, but she wouldn't let it go. It then began to annoy me. It's kind of like tickling. Somebody tries to tickle you, and it's cute, and you laugh for a second, but when they don't stop, it turns into something else. You're ready to punch them. Just sayin'. It's all fun and games until someone gets punched.

Now let's assess your situation: This one is especially friend-specific. Some friends thrive on practical jokes, but have you ever gone too far? Did you see the twinge in your friend's face as the joke went down? Were you paying attention? If you are in the early stages of friendship you may not know where the line is. If you have gone too far, they will in some way let you know. Pay attention. The first thing to do is apologize. Explain why you thought they might have thought that would be funny and make sure it never happens again.

CHAPTER 5

Thou Shall Never Put Your Friend in a Compromising Position

"I would rather be alone with dignity than in a relationship that requires me to sacrifice my self-respect"

—Mandy Hale

Truth, trust, staying in touch,
with no humiliation to come,
and uncompromising values
are ties that bind together.

Sometimes we get ourselves in a real jam. We know we need help, and our first thoughts are of our friend. That's a good thought. We know our friends will do whatever they can to help us out of a jam. But never, ever, ask a friend to do something that goes against what they believe or against their personal value system.

This is another situation you may not be able to come back from. For example, I don't lie. So, if someone were to ask me to lie for them, it would make me wonder if they really knew me. It would make me wonder if they were really my friend. It would make me wonder *"What is wrong with you?"* Some people lie all the time and lying for a friend would not go against their value system. They would actually see it as being helpful. What I have come to know is, like I have said before, the truth *always rises to the top*, and the consequences of a lie may fall heavier than what you can carry. It tests your integrity. Do you have it? Do you have the moral compass that rises under challenging conditions?

I've heard people say, that if you lie, you cheat, and if you cheat, you steal, and if you steal, you are a liar and a cheat who may kill. I don't know if that is absolutely true but compromising your values can lead you further into devaluing your principles than you ever intended to go. Don't go there. Don't get on that road.

None of these characteristics are what you want in a friend. Knowing you have a friend like this would be a cause to pause when it comes to trust. Lying for you, cheating for you, and taking the blame for you, is a place you should never ask or allow a friend to go. It's your friend. Never let them compromise their values for you. They may be put in an uncomfortable position because of their relationship with you, but you are not supposed to be the one who puts them there. They may love you enough to go there, but you love them enough not to let them. Things of this nature absolutely put a strain on the relationship.

People who put their friends in compromising positions, well let's just say they may need to go into the acquaintance file. I'm not saying, they absolutely need to be moved down the ladder, but there is definitely cause to think about it. There is something in them that has disconnected from you.

Now, can you cheat for them in monopoly? Maybe slip them an extra five hundred dollars under the table? Hmmm..., Well, perhaps if you tell the other people at the end of the game what you did, but only tell them if you lose. If you win, you will have to refer to the secrets chapter, then, to the truth chapter. After all that, you will find it's probably easier to just lose with grace.

Now let's assess your situation: Has a friend ever asked you to do something that compromised your values? If so, how did it make you feel? Did you ever ask your friend to do something that went against their values? This is one of those things that you have to look at and decide whether this friend is one who may need to be adjusted in the friendship ladder. This issue speaks to the character of a person. It speaks to who you and they really are. If something like this has happened in your relationship it is something that definitely has to be discussed. You have to decide if this person should be that involved in your life.

CHAPTER 6

Thou Shall Always Remember a Friend's Special Days

"The heart that truly loves, never forgets"

—Indian Proverb

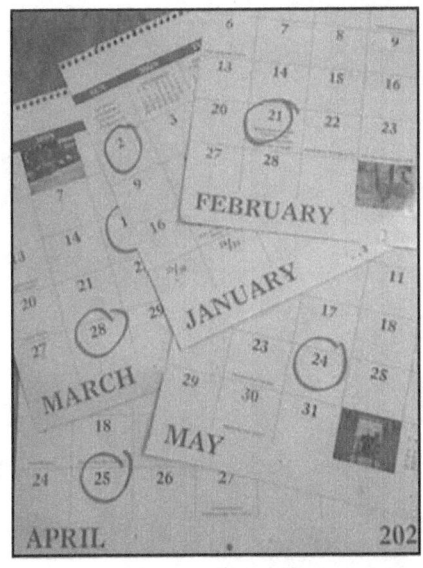

Truth, trust, staying in touch,
with no humiliation to come,
not compromising values,
remembering the times,
makes you one of a kind.

Remembering the days that are special to a friend is important. Though we may not forget a particular circumstance, the actual day it occurred may escape us. So, simply write it down. Remember when that special day is coming up. When you do this, you are being mindful of the emotional state of your friend. People have triggers that change their emotional state, and knowing what has happened in their past and when it happened will help you navigate through these emotions.

Whether the day is a happy occasion like a birthday, a wedding anniversary, or a new life situation, or a sad occasion like a death or a breakup, it is irrelevant. It doesn't matter what the day is, just be aware it may be important to your friend. On those days, a friend may want you to help celebrate with them or be a shoulder to cry on. What is important to them is important to you because *they* are important to you. You may not have the same emotional attachment to the situation, but you have an emotional attachment to your friend.

Your friend will appreciate it when you call to say, "How are we celebrating this?" or "I just wanted to see how you were doing today." A simple gesture like this is the difference between everyone else and a friend. My friend lost her husband, and I made sure I wrote down that date. I wanted her to know that I would never forget what she lost. It is important to me that I am there for her at that time. Because we are hundreds of miles apart, I call her. If I lived close, I would be at her door. So, I call her anytime around that date to check on her. It will get easier for her as time goes on, but it's important that I walk that time out with her. Remembering special days makes *you* special. It makes you special because you were mindful of your friend. It shows you pay attention and that you care.

Unfortunately, these "special days" could entail you having to do some very uncomfortable things. Your friend may ask you to commemorate or celebrate in odd ways. You're the friend, so you gotta do it and do it with a straight face. Your role is not to question why. Your role is simply to stand by your friend's side. Now, you may have to be the voice of reason. When Jazmine Sullivan sang, "I broke the windows out your car", and Carrie Underwood sang, "I took a Louisville slugger to both headlights", they never talk about the possibility of going to jail. Believe me, when I say, you *will* go to jail! You may have to talk them down off the ledge, and buy some darts and throw them at an old picture of the one who broke their heart instead. Maybe eat some cake and ice cream. Always hide the bats, guns, and knives on these types of days. You are not Thelma and Louise.

Now let's assess your situation. Do you know the significant dates in your friend's life? If you don't know, why don't you? Is it that you forgot? Or did you not think to remember? Did you think it wasn't important to remember the date, just the incident? Maybe your friend doesn't care if you remember dates. Maybe your friend doesn't want to remember a date at all. You should know which and follow that path.

CHAPTER 7

Thou Shall Remember Your Friend's Favorites

"Oh my goodness, you remembered"

—unknown

Truth, trust, staying in touch, with no humiliation to come, not compromising values, remembering the times, remembering the favorites, it shows you care, shows you're dedicated.

Remembering your friends' favorites is also one of those things that make *you* special. It is not a must-do, but it is a bonus. It simply means you pay attention and remember. It's a nice feeling when someone knows you well enough to know that even though you don't wear it much, your favorite color is yellow, and though you don't cook it much, your favorite dish is lasagna. Whenever I visit my friend who lives hundreds of miles away from me, she puts yellow roses in my bathroom because she knows that's my favorite flower. She bakes oatmeal and raisin cookies for me because that's my favorite cookie, and most likely, before I leave, one of the dinners will be lasagna because that's my favorite dish. Her doing these things is very precious to me. It shows her love for me and a desire to make me feel good. Isn't that what you want and what you want for your friend? Isn't that the most basic level of a good relationship, making them feel good and making them feel good about being your friend?

Simple gestures become enormous steps in creating a closer friendship. You don't have to like their favorites. Their favorites may be nasty, ugly, sound stupid, and be boring to you. But your responsibility is to know when it's needed, how to make it, where to get it, or where to go see it.

Let me add a little extra here. It would be excellent if you remember what it is they are allergic to also. There is nothing worse than bringing something in that blows your friend up like a basketball, turns them into a rashed out tomato, or worse, stops them from breathing. (*Stopping your friend from breathing would not be a good thing. I'm just sayin…*) If you can't remember, just write it down.

Now let's assess your situation. Have you ever said you didn't like something to your friend and they never remember or they ignore it? If so, how did that make you feel? Have *you* forgotten something your friend felt you should know? How did that feel? I say again, these things are just added specialties from a close friend. But you have to find out how important that is to your friend. It may mean more to them than it does to you. If so, how do you handle that? Simply, if you care enough about them, you will not minimize their feelings about something.

CHAPTER 8

✦

Thou Shall Like Your Friend as Well as Love Them

"Because of you, I laugh a little harder,
cry a little less and smile a lot more"

—unknown

Truth, trust, staying in touch, with no
humiliation to come, not compromising values,
remembering the times, remembering the
favorites, like and love are ties from above.

When you live as a Christian, the Bible instructs you to love everyone. There are no stipulations. Just love everyone with the love of God and treat them kindly with that same love. It doesn't matter who they are, where they come from, or how they act. Just love them. So, to say that you *love* someone doesn't necessarily mean you *like* them. Nowhere did I read that you had to like them. (Please tell me if I missed a scripture somewhere.) To love them with the love of God is deliberate. To be kind to them is intentional. Often it is an "in-spite-of" action. God's love is unconditional. So, we love when it is easy, and we love when it is difficult. But *liking* someone is something else all together.

Liking someone is an involuntary thing. It just is. It has nothing to do with love at all, and it has everything to do with the character and personality of that person who they are and how they will draw you to them. The compatibility of their nature with yours is what makes for comfortable and harmonious interactions. It is an unmanufactured ease. It is a flow like water falling over a ledge. It just happens. You usually can point to specifics of why you like them. "I like them because they're kind," or "they're funny," or "they're compassionate."

Every now and then you need to tell your friend why you like them. That's a point of being intentional. We all know someone we "love", and we can point to things we really don't "like" about them. We don't want to spend much time with them because whatever those things are, they are going to come out, and we don't want to be around for it. We end up saying, "But I still love 'em."

Have you ever met someone and your first impression of them is, "I wouldn't mind spending more time with this person", or "They're pretty cool." You didn't have to put any effort into your feelings. You didn't have to remind yourself to be nice. I do have to admit that sometimes, I have to remind myself to be kind to a person. I have to show them intentional love. They are one of God's creations.

This is not to say that you can't develop a friendship with someone who at first impression, you do not like. It is a possibility. Maybe when you first met them, they were having a bad day. Perhaps they weren't feeling well or got some bad news, and they weren't handling it well. So many different scenarios could be playing out that you aren't aware of. Then, when you see them again, you're thinking, *"Why didn't I like this person?"* You could become great friends. Maybe if you talk, talk, talk, you will find out what went wrong during that first interaction.

But often, the first impression you have of someone may be exactly right. There is always a way to be kind even when you are having a bad day. If a person hasn't figured that out, that may not be a person you want to get close to.

Most friendships begin with a genuine like for one another. The reason you begin to spend more time with a person is because you "like" them. That time together is creating the friendship. Have you ever seen two supposed friends together and one is acting like an idiot and the other is rolling their eyes at them? Do you wonder why they're friends? Are you questioning the relationship? It seems like one doesn't like the other. One, a friend would calm the idiotness. Two, the idiot would not be giving idiotness, causing their friend to be embarrassed. I know idiotness is not a word but sometimes you have to make up words because the real ones just don't describe what you really want to say. Just sayin… Dah!

If a person is a friend, you want to like them! Otherwise, what's the point? Who wants to be around someone they don't even like? Don't be that person. Don't be someone who strives to be friends with someone they don't really like because they are a person of status, or because you feel that being friends with then helps you fit in with a certain group of people. Don't make that compromise. That's not friendship.

Having a friend is to have someone you want to share things with, do things with, talk to, go places with, and have good times with. It's a person who, in turn, wants to share these things with you. Who wants to do all that with someone they don't even like? Again, dah! Bottom line, if you don't like them, they are not friend material. You have nothing to even begin a tie with.

Now, let's asses your situation. Simply, do you like them? What do you like about them? Name three different things about them that make you smile. You may want to reach out and ask them, "Do you like *me*?"

CHAPTER 9

Thou Shall Always Act Like A Friend

"Your friend is your field which you sow with
love and reap with thanksgiving"

—Khalil Gibran

Forever the friend,
always until the end.

Time will pass on. Your children will grow up and move on with their own lives. Your life will change in some way every season. If you are blessed enough to live a long time, you will have many ups and downs, and twists and turns. Having that one constant in your life will make every change so much easier. Whether it's two or three good friends or just one very special one, stay close to them. Old age is wonderful if there is an old age friend walking next to you.

The only way to have a good friend is to be a good friend. You can't have a friendship without a relationship. A relationship is a state of connectedness between people. It can't be one-sided. Otherwise, one is losing. One may even be used.

No matter what the situation, a friend should never have to question their position. Sometimes it's hard, but you always prove yourself to be a friend. You're the one who takes up for them, covers their short-comings, and makes them look good in public. I sing, and I have friends who sing back-up for me. I have some short-comings and some flaws, and they take great care not to let them show. They cover them for me. Where I falter, they stay steady. That's what we are to our friends, a steadiness they can count on.

You hold your friend's hand when they're afraid and encourage them when they're frustrated. You wipe away their tears when they're sad and laugh out loud with them when things are going well. You celebrate their triumphs and boast in all their good. You pick them up when they fall and hold them up when they're weak. You're the one who makes the good times bigger and better and the bad times pass by just a little quicker and a little easier. You forgive them quickly and don't recall it later. I have to say that again. *You forgive them quickly.* Take no account for a suffered wrong. In other words, don't keep a list of offenses. Sometimes, even our friends may say something or do something that offends us.

I remember this happening to me. I said to myself, "Mary, remember who this is. This is your friend. You know their heart. They never mean to offend you. Forgive them, and let it go." Their motive was not to hurt me in any way. They were only speaking their truth, what they truly believed. When needed, you may have to speak about the issue that caused the offense or hurt to get clarity on both sides. But there are times when it is unnecessary, and it is then that you just let it go.

At times you may lay down your own life for them. What does this statement mean? Do you physically die for them? Let's hope that choice never has to be made. But what I mean in this case, is putting your own situations, desires, and feelings aside while you "stand in the gap" for them. You are there for them until whatever is wrong is right again. International gospel singer Babbie Mason has a beautiful song that speaks directly to this. It is appropriately called "Standing in the Gap." You always hold them close. Literally! You are their safe place. You tell them of all that is good about them and remind them they are reverently and wonderfully made by God. You love them at all times.

Remember, "Love endures long and is patient and kind; Love is never envious, nor boils over in jealousy," Love bears up under anything and everything that comes, it is ever ready to believe the best of a person, its hopes are fadeless under all circumstances, and it endures all things without weakening." (I Cor. 13 4, 7–Amp). Isn't that how we want someone to love us?

No matter what else is going on around them, no matter what anyone else is doing, no matter what else they may see, when they look into your eyes, they should always see, **A FRIEND**.

Now let's assess your situation: Do you have a friend? Are *you* a friend?

THE PROVERBS OF FRIENDSHIP

"A friend loves at all times, and a
brother is born for adversity"

—Proverbs 17:17

"Faithful are the wounds of a friend, but
the kisses of an enemy are deceitful"

—Proverbs 27:6

"Oil and perfume make a heart glad;
So does the sweetness of a friend's
counsel that comes from the heart"

—Proverbs 27:9

"My command is this; love each other as I have loved you. Greater love has no man than this that he lay down his life for his friends."

—John 15:12-13

Remember:

Friend: _____

Birthday: _____

Favorite color: _____

Favorite food: _____

Dislikes: _____

Allergy: _____

Days to remember: _____

Remember:

Friend: _____

Birthday: _____

Favorite color: _____

Favorite food: _____

Dislikes: _____

Allergy: _____

Days to remember: _____

Remember:

Friend: _____

Birthday: _____

Favorite color: _____

Favorite food: _____

Dislikes: _____

Allergy: _____

Days to remember: _____

Remember:

Friend: _____

Birthday: _____

Favorite color: _____

Favorite food: _____

Dislikes: _____

Allergy: _____

Days to remember: _____

ABOUT THE AUTHOR

My husband passed away when our son was just twenty-two months old and one month from my thirtieth birthday. To say my life was turned upside down would be an understatement. For a long time I felt like I was living outside my body. I was taking care of all of my responsibilities, going to work  and working a lot of hours, leading the devotion at my church and taking care of my son. But, I was feeling nothing.

Because of the relationships I had formed, I had great friends who helped walk me through it all. They didn't just ask if I was alright, they made sure I was. My best friend, who lived 6 hours away, would call and tell me to come and visit her for a few days. While I was there she was such a nurturer. She took care of me. When I came back home I could breathe again. While I was home my other friend was always checking on me and to this day continues to make sure I'm alright. And I am. God gave them to me. I say that a friend is the hand of God reaching down to touch your life. Every time I see them, I see Him.

I believe in friendship. I believe we all need true friendships. I believe when we have them we have a blessing from God.

Contact the author at:
MWitherspoon1214@gmail.com

www.ingramcontent.com/pod-product-compliance
Lightning Source LLC
Chambersburg PA
CBHW031231120626
46545CB00003B/1083